BLOOM

A Journey to Self-Love

BLOOM

A Journey to Self-Love

-Poetry & Prose-

Brittany Travesté

TQP Press | New Orleans

BLOOM: A JOURNEY TO SELF-LOVE

TQP Press
New Orleans, LA

www.brittanytraveste.com

Cover Art by Alvin Epps
Alvinepps.com

Interior Art by Jade Meyers
Jade1991.com

Edited by Erika Murray
Poeticallyspeakingpublishing.com

ISBN 978-0-692-82922-6

All definitions referenced are taken from the Merriam-Webster Online Dictionary © 2017 by Merriam-Webster.

For the mother who planted audacity into the soil of her daughter's spirit.

STAGES

Preface

"If you feel lost, disappointed, hesitant, or weak, return to yourself, to who you are, here and now and when you get there, you will discover yourself, like a lotus flower in full bloom, even in a muddy pond, beautiful and strong." — Masaru Emoto, *Secret Life of Water*

One gazes at a flower in a market or garden and neglects to think about how it came to be. The only concern is that it is beautiful. Yet, there is beauty in the becoming, too; as much as there is pain, doubt and confusion. The flower that you see underwent a transformation. It began as a seed, and that seed held within it, all of the magic that it would ever need; but it had to learn this. Before it could bloom, it had to sprout, and it had to grow. It had to look within and allow itself to be just as wonderful as it was created to be—no matter the conditions that surrounded it.

We have so much in common with flowers.

We, however, attempt to hide the process. We try to pretend that we woke up in love with ourselves. As if our mothers pushed us out into a world that is perfect. We like to have others believe that we always make the right choices. We want it to seem as if we don't break sometimes, like we don't bruise.

We can no longer afford to keep up with this façade. People are watching, believing, and holding themselves to impossible standards because of it.

I am a woman, who has come alive—who has tapped into her magic— because of my shortcomings and failures. A tainted perception of love, an inability to truly see my worth, and the refusal to stare into the face of my own demons have all worked together to stunt my growth. No more of this.

Like many women, I have, at times, relied on a man's admiration instead of my own. I have put the attainment of a romantic relationship before nurturing the union with myself. I have granted my flesh the permission to control me. I have allowed the opinions of others to trump my own. I have permitted woes from childhood to ravage my adult life. I have given guilt the permission to sweat from my pores. And after swimming, drowning, and resurfacing in the Mess-I-Made Ocean, I found that I am sufficient all by my damn self. Regardless of the mistakes of my past, I am worthy.

On this journey to love, I've realized that I have within me all that I've ever needed—just like the flower. I don't wish to be perceived as just another beautiful thing. There is ugliness here, too, and I am blooming in spite of it. Truth is, I am blooming because of it.

Through this collection of poetry, prose, and honest reflection, I aim to lay myself bare so that you can choose to bloom, too. Through my vulnerability, I desire for you to embrace the highs and lows of your journey to self-love and not omit one petal.

Brittany Travesté
New Orleans, LA
November 2016

1

Seed

\sēd\

noun

1.

a flowering plant's unit of reproduction, capable of developing into another such plant

2.

the source or beginning of something which continues to develop or grow

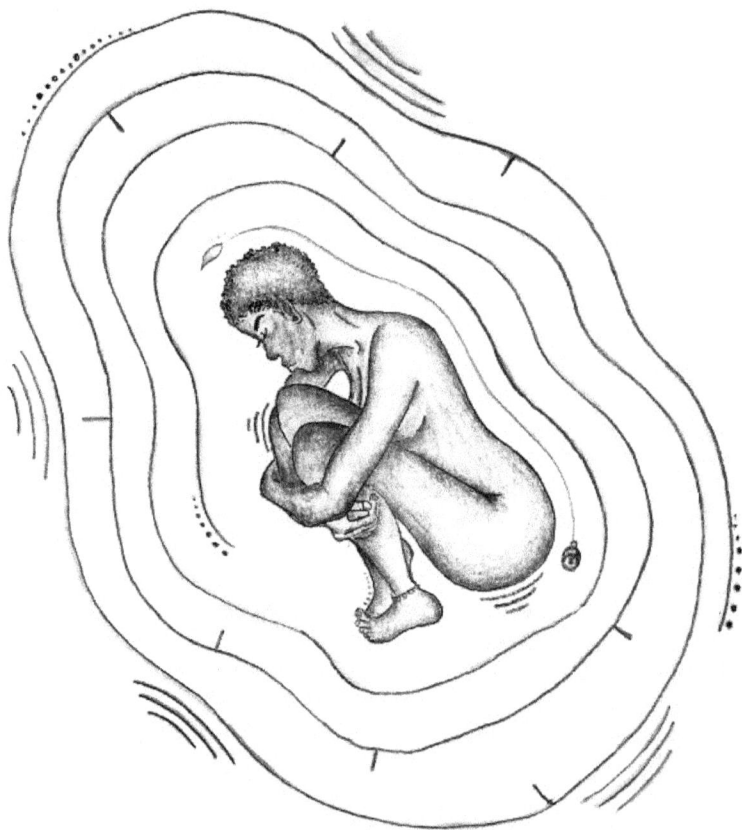

Daydreaming and I'm Thinking of You

Just as most little girls, I used to fantasize about the man I'd one day marry and the children that I'd bear for him. I imagined that by now, I'd be staring love in the face, whispering nothings, drenched with honey, before bed. And there'd be little ones with eyes as bright as mine and skin as dark as the man I'd choose, running in at dawn. In my maturity, I recognize that life rarely plays out the way you plan it, and well, it just isn't that simple.

When the time arises, dream, will you come true for me?

The wide-eyed, pig-tailed little girl within me has already named them both in sweet expectation: Lily and Luna, for the earthly, yet divinely crafted things I cherish.

Green

soft rain
unripe fruit
the tenderness of your touch
innocence
my childhood
summer runs through the park
youthful expressions
naivety
crisp grass
caterpillars crossing concrete thresholds
stains on my jeans that mama couldn't wash out
daddy's '76 Chevy Chevelle
grandma's collards
oak trees
eucalyptus hand soap
friendships in bloom
forgotten picnics with old lovers
strings of daisies orbiting my head
budding romance
saturdays in spring
holding your hand
first kiss
morning dew
damp leaves between my toes
fresh air
God's design
serenity
renewal
life

I Wonder

I was never bold enough to ask, but if I could...

>What was holding you back?

>Why did you allow them to silence you?

>Why did you so willingly relinquish your control?

>Who are you, under the smile that you wear for me?

>What kind of woman would you choose to be had I not been born?

What do *you* want?

Insecurities, but Thank God for Mama

She can't dance; no rhythm at all.
Her nose is too wide.
She can't double-dutch; can't even hop-scotch.
Can't play numbers or throw jacks.
She's too skinny. No booty. Flat chest.
She's too tall. She's too proper. She's too nerdy.
Glasses always crooked.
She dresses like a white girl.
Her hair isn't long enough.

My mama said I was beautiful though.

Irony

She waited for you
to protect her.
She blamed herself
for your rejection,
thinking the denial
was somehow her fault.

She never told a soul
about your inadequacies
as a parent.
She couldn't understand
why she wanted to safeguard
you.

You are the reason that she
still cannot look at herself
in the mirror
without getting sick
to her stomach.

Older now, her body is a house
that is broken in
and empty.
Her pride is boarded up;
her self-esteem shows
signs of decay.

There is a man who finds her.
He desires to love her;
attempts to offer his shield.

She does not deem herself worthy.

What Could Have Been

My daddy was a dream that many women fell asleep holding. They conjured him up; let him run wild in their imaginations. Sadly, those illusions were nothing like the real thing. Only in a trance, could he give them the love that they needed.

I'd watch them come and go.

Womanish

I wanted to know
what it was like
to be held
by a man,
like the women
in those books
that I had
no business
reading.

What a murderer curiosity is;
killed the cat
and
my innocence.

Trust Issues

I stood there.
Bags packed,
waiting on you,
for hours.

You never came.

How in the world am I to trust another man's word?

Lessons from Divorce

Before my mother made the decision to leave her first husband, she asked my 10-year-old self what I thought *we* should do. My response to her: *Leave.*

I learned three lessons from this:

1. If you are unhappy, leave.
2. Your children watch your every move. They, too, are affected by your bad choices in love.
3. It is important to have a voice and to deny what does not fit you.

Defense Mechanisms

Her hips
might not be growing
as quickly as theirs,
but her mouth sure is swift.
That little girl
has an attitude on her.

11

Sprout

\sprout\

verb

1.

to begin to grow; shoot forth, as a plant from a seed

2.

to develop or grow quickly

The New Girl

So, you're at a middle school in Jackson, Mississippi
and the girls don't care for you because
well, you're new
and you're cute
and their boys do
and you got that special thing about you
that New Orleans accent
that high head in the sky
that bright skin
that little switch when you walk
but you're going on thirteen
and their words sting like
alcohol on a scraped knee

you don't let them know, though.

Instead you flirt back with their boyfriends
you come to school extra fly
you mouth off,
knowing damn well
that you've never had a fight
you propel what that they think they already know about you
and you can't wait to get back to New Orleans.

Playing Dumb

Being smart doesn't make the boys like you and it doesn't make the cool kids want to hang out with you. But, woe is me. I can't hide this gifted mind or these honors classes. I always end up slipping up and letting the nerd out, like 'actually, the square root of 144 is 12.'

Damn.

Daddy's Little Girl

My father died three days after I turned 16.

The moment replays in my mind
like a broken record
scratching at my soul
each time I decide to "go there."

My mother picks me up from school
with an absent look in her eyes,
and I could tell that tears were the culprit
for smearing her mascara.

During the ride to my grandparents' house,
I rack my mind with the possibilities
of what could be urgent enough
to disrupt learning
and cause her to cry.

The silent voyage ends.
We get out of the car.
She blurts out
that my daddy
has been murdered,
that my daddy
is no longer alive.

That my daddy
has been stolen away from me
and will no longer be around to
excitedly scream out baby girl
when he sees me
and that I won't be able to run into his arms.

Time stands still
my world stops spinning
I begin to fall to the ground
my grandfather catches me.

Selfish questions like
who will purchase my first car
who will give me that extra 50 dollars
when mama and stepdad say no
who will tell me that the boy around the corner is not
good enough for his daughter
who will take me on road trips in an apple green Chevy
who will walk me down the aisle

Angry questions like
why did I spend so much time being mad at him
why did it take me so long to forgive broken promises
why did I still blame him for the pain he caused my mother
who in the hell would take a father away from his daughters
why in the fuck would he choose to live a life of uncertainty
when he was my little sister's hero
when he had people who depended on him
when he had people who loved him
when I loved him

They said that in his bedroom,
my 3rd quarter report card
laid on the nightstand.

And you ask me why I can so easily heal from a breakup?

My father died three days after I turned 16,
but it wasn't the first time
he had broken
my heart.

High School Sweetheart

My first love was exquisite.
Milk chocolate delight
athletic build
popular in the city
and he saw me as a prize,
beautiful
and innocent.

He liked that I cared about my schoolwork,
loved that I hadn't been around the block.
And I liked the way he put me
on pedestals,
the way he trophied me.

He bragged about me to his Catholic school friends
and on those rare occasions
that he reached out
to pick me up
and spend a little time,
he showed me off.
You know, we walked side
by side
at those high school dances.

This tickled my ego.
I delighted in the idea that
there was a guy who all the girls wanted,
who wanted me,
who chose me
to share his darkest secrets
and his fears.

So we shared, and we laughed,
and we fought, and we cried,
and we loved
as deeply as our budding
hearts knew how to.

But we were seniors in high school, and
the time was ticking
and our hope was dying
because life was
bringing us
in different directions.

We broke up before college,
thinking that our young love
wouldn't be able to survive the distance.
He stayed in Louisiana, and
I went off to DC.
Against our better judgment,
we didn't let go right away.
I kept myself pure for him, and
he said that he would do the same, but
there were girls he tried to hide from me,
and then vengeful actions
to make him feel how I felt.
We caused enough damage in those first few months
to completely destroy any semblance of optimism
that remained.

For years, I compared every person I dated
to him.
It took a long time
to let go of the dream
that we'd be together in the end.

I'll always love him though.

Twinkle, Twinkle Little Star
Let Me Tell You Who *You* Are
A Lullaby Revisited

Of all the stars
in the night sky
I chose you
To guide me,
to light my
darkness,
to fill
empty spaces.

But you,
in all of your splendor,
you couldn't
and you wouldn't
twinkle just for me.

And in all of my selfishness,
I couldn't
and I wouldn't
accept that.

See I needed to own you
to belong to you
I needed you
to have freedom of choice
and to still choose me.

So I let you go
so that you could be plentiful,
and to the Moon I ran.

Tears in my eyes,
I cried to her,
"Why won't he shine
 just for me?"

In all of her wisdom,
she replied
"Honey, love
is not about ownership,
and there is no need
to grieve
over the light of another.
There is a love
that is grander.
One that will glisten
for you
brighter than any other can."

"Please Moon,
point him out to me,"
I begged.

She responded,
"Darling, that light
is inside of *you*."

"Billie's Song: A Blues Story"

"Good morning heartache, you old gloomy sight. Good morning heartache. Thought we said goodbye last night. I tossed and turned until it seemed you had gone, but here you are with the dawn." *

~ ~ ~

Billie Holiday's tune had become native to my being, residing in the deepest parts of me. I was beginning to forget that I had never known the tortured soul, that I didn't coax her to sing it or to tell the world of our shared misfortunes in love. The words took on a life of their own, and I was the afflicted one who mirrored the sad melody and embodied its sorrow. Now that I think of it, the song had been haunting me since the first time I heard it.

In my youth, Nanna often played it for me on the old, faithful Victrola that her beloved uncle had given to her as a gift on her 12th birthday. Being a collector of sorts, she preserved the antique through the years, and flocked to it whenever nostalgia called. I would sit in the frail wooden chair at her kitchen table, with the smell of red beans simmering on the stove, while she braided my thick, untamed hair—my mother didn't believe in relaxing potions. I recall her slender fingers with red nail polish moving ever so swiftly, as she told tales of her blossoming years.

She was a silk-crowned mulatto girl, growing up in New Orleans during a time when jazz music was the only choice, and it meant *everything* if it didn't have the swing. It was a period where black folk busied themselves with drinking and dancing to ignore the woes of segregation; though in New Orleans, life was a little bit sweeter for those of mixed ancestry.

I recall one occasion, her long, grey hair, brushing my shoulder as she bent towards me to tell me about the infamous, Mr. André. As Nanna

23

reminisced on love gone sour, Billie sung her song. Her pained utterance floated from the phonograph and hovered over Nanna and me, an astronomic rain cloud reminding her and enlightening me of what tainted love can do to a soul. I can remember the moment vividly.

"Nanna, what's heartache?" I asked.

She laughed.

"Nina, before I met your grandfather, I loved a man by the name of Louis André. He used to take me dancing every weekend and give me the loveliest magnolia flowers. He tried real hard to be a good man to me, but he just wasn't cut out for no serious lovin,' at least not the kind of love that I needed—sanctified and scorching, all at once. I loved that man with conviction, but so did the rest of the lady folk in this part of Louisiana. And Louis sought out to fill every need. He tried to hide his two-timing ways from me, but I found out eventually. It broke my spirit something terrible."

"Why'd he do that to you?" I asked. At that moment, in all of my nine-year-old glory and naivety, I decided that men were snakes that you needed to be cautious of. This applied to my father, too, who chose to skip out soon after I was conceived. He did not disappear completely, around periodically to teach me the highs and lows of life in a way that only a biological dad—not necessarily father—can. I realized, early on, his natural gift for playing both villain and saint; I guess the same can be said for all human beings.

"Child, who knows why these men do what they do," said Nanna. "Us women sometimes bear the unimaginable and still manage to believe in love. But, that was long before your grandfather came into my life. He proved to be the other that my spirit had always been searching for."

"Well, I hate boys," I said. "And I'm never going to fall in love."

"Ha! Is that right?" she said. "One day, you'll be singing a different tune."

24

I remember her looking out of her window, through the ivory lace curtains, past the brightly colored shotgun houses that lined the lower 9th ward neighborhood, and out into the sky. Maybe she looked to find my grandfather there. My mother was just sixteen when the tobacco took his lungs and the years of hard Southern labor got the best of him. I wish I could have met him. Nanna told me that I received my spunky ways from him. I always wondered where my adventurous spirit arose.

My mother was so reserved and set in her ways. Being an only child, I got the brunt of her wrath. I was always getting scolded for venturing too far away from the house. *The giant willow trees down past the Nelsons' front gate called to me.* And getting rebuked for coloring on my white bedroom walls. *I felt that life should be colorful and vibrant as opposed to bare.* But what bothered me most was my mother's opposition to my Nanna being so open with me.

"Your grandmother has no business sharing those things with you. You're too young to understand," she would say.

After a while, I stopped telling her what Nanna and I talked about during my weekend visits. I lived for those conversations with Nanna and would not lose them because my mother wanted to keep me wide-eyed and trusting.

I believe that the talks with my grandmother in her tiny kitchen with its mix-match appliances and comforting floral wallpaper, while Lady Day sang the blues, were a forewarning of sorts. Though, as the lives of many strong women have shown, all logic and caution is thrown out of the nearest window when love, of the enchanting disposition, enters the door.

It amazes me that at nine, I had more resolve than my now 25-year-old self who is caught up in a debilitating affair with my *own* Louis André. It's almost like I forgot about the pain that Billie sung of, like my vow to never fall in love slipped from my memory. If only I could talk to Nanna, now. She could help me to recall my strength. Tell me how to get over. Teach me how to say goodbye to heartache and let go of this damn song.

~ ~ ~

"Good morning heartache, here we go again. Good morning heartache, you're the one who knew me when. I might as well get used to you hanging around. Good morning heartache, sit down." *

* Billie Holiday "Good Morning Heartache" © 1946 Sony/ATV Music Publishing LLC

111

Grow

\ grō\

Verb

1.

(of a living thing) to undergo natural development by increasing in size and changing physically; progress to maturity

2.

to become better or improved in some way

3.

to come to be by degrees; become

Blues in His Left Thigh

I mean...
I was Bessie, Coltrane, King, Holiday, Scott, Etta, Rainey, and
Marsalis.
I was bebop.
I was swing.
I blues-ed him and bruised him.
I was bright, full moon
and blood orange dawn.
I night danced and morning fed him.
I was collard greens with pig fat in his belly
and salt water in his eyes.
I was the earth that shook him,
made him contemplate the error in his ways.
I mean, I broke this brotha down
and built him anew.

Had his mood indigo,
his nose wide
Had him musing over the alleys of his mind
Asking how
Asking why
Thanking God.
We were soul speaking 'round midnight.
Had him diggin' the funk enough to fill me,
Make my womb round with life.
Had him forgetting who it was that came before me.
"Was it Erin?
Was it Deshawna?
Dada dada doodoo doop."
He was gone.

The detangling of this woman
who stood before him
intrigued him.

Made him want to dive deeper
so that he could grasp
 the origins of this ocean
This peculiar entity,
this contradiction of everything
he ever thought he knew
about love.
He asked himself
what pulls me to her
the way the moon
beckons the tide
to earth's shore.
I derailed him with need.
He was moonstruck.

And still,
it wasn't enough to keep him.

Regret

But I was the one who called this off, right?
Stood with arms crossed
and indifference eclipsing my being
the way the moon covers the sun.

Gave the reasons I was done,
this time.

Because the last time
this little girl cried wolf,
you stood before the door.
You wouldn't allow it.

Yet, this time,
unlike the last time,
you didn't stop me.

I watched you walk to your car.
I heard you say goodnight,
and it felt final.

Stepping back into the house,
I reassured myself that I made the right choice.
The fallacy gave me enough confidence to stand up straight
and that feeling lasted for days.

But tonight,
the music won't groove.
The drinks won't numb.
Laughter won't reach my soul.
I sit here with a phone that won't ring,
remembering,
that I was the one who called this off.

Since We're Being Honest...

Sometimes the loneliness settles into my bones and I become unable to move.

Truth or Dare

Truth?

You were not ready to be respected and treated like a "queen" when dating the last guy. Let's keep it real. You wanted things fast. You wanted to be touched. Wanted your physical needs met. Wanted to forego foundation building and just dive in. But he was old-school. He wanted to wait for you, pray with you, and hold you higher. Wanted to introduce you to friends, bring you home to mama. He saw grace in you and a future with you. But your girls called him boring, and you let their judgment overshadow his virtues.

The next guy? Yeah, he was more grounded than a few of your other lovers, but the actual compatibility between you and him was overlooked because he was able to please your body. He moved it just good enough, hit the spot just right enough, and fucked your mind just cloudy enough for you to settle for him. The funny thing is that he didn't last either. He left you and your body broken.

Why, dear, do you allow your vagina to make decisions for your heart?

Wardrobe Malfunction

And I think I wore this very same outfit the last time the pain of losing you undressed my feelings and sent me running home for cover.

Yet, I let you back in.

And I put this damn dress on.

So, who's really to blame for my tears?

Lily and Luna,

Sometimes your mama wondered if she'd ever birth you, the way she'd love them and then send them on with the breeze.

Pinky Promise

And it wasn't the commitments you made
It wasn't the resolutions that I couldn't maintain
It wasn't even the promises that we didn't keep
It was me looking at myself in the mirror
saying what I would never do again,
that I did anyway.
It was that I compromised myself.
Allowed your dirty hands to touch my body,
when Lord knows you didn't even deserve to breathe my air.

Lost Ones

I do
solemnly swear
that breaking up
with a sista friend
is a pain
far worse
than what
any loss of a man
could ever bring.

Thirst Trap

You left me thirsting,
clenching my throat
wishing to remember who the hell I was before you.
Dying to drink an elixir to fix the brokenness

How did I get here?

No Strings Attached

This was supposed to be easy.

No cute pictures to delete from Instagram pages
No cell phone wallpaper to change
No watches or cologne to return
No oversized t-shirts to stuff into the back of a small drawer
No mothers or big sisters to disappoint
No colleagues to explain the break up to

We kept pieces of ourselves from the other,
trying to save hearts.

Yet, mine still bleeds.

Weariness

Tonight, I just want to slide out of my pain, pull it over my head, and hang it in the closet where all skeletons are said to be.

I know, one day, I'll have to face it and clean it, like mamas do.

But tonight, I am tired.

Insecurities Live in This House

Sometimes I, too, feel the heaviness of darkness that swallows one whole and repeatedly whispers "you are not enough."

Insanity

if i was still sane, i'd recall
that ain't shit you got
good enough to keep me
drowning
in an ocean
of so-called love
knowing damn well that i can't swim.

> But i've lost my mind
> And here i am
> sinking.

> Ain't that some shit?

The Body Knows

Constipation
flu
stomach virus
sneezing
coughing
headache
insomnia
fatigue
lack of appetite
elevated temperatures
nausea
wooziness
clinic visits
blood tests

My body knew that you were no good before I did.

Wasn't Enough

You spread yourself across my bread
Doubled yourself over at my command
Kneeled down on your knees in reverence,
at the foot of my bed.

And still I chose to lie with another.

"An Unquenchable Appetite"

For months, I denied myself his presence. Not wanting to initiate a run-in with karma. Not wanting to ruin my relationship. Not wanting to give in to the ruthless, self-indulging part of myself. Not wanting to admit how unhappy and dissatisfied I was with my life. Yet there I was on New Year's Eve, that symbolic day set aside for resolution and reflection, on my way to him. This was the only choice.

It was a cloudless winter day, with a soft breeze picking up frivolous things in the street that once mattered, as I drove past monotonous brown brick row houses. Palms sweating, I continued to drive despite my anxiety. On the highway, the trees showed no sign of life. No flowers. No leaves. Just dry, brittle branches. I felt like they resembled the woman I had become while living there in DC.

Through my car window, the sunlight was dazzling and exploiting, illuminating all of my iniquity. I was unable to hide any longer. As the film in my head kept my attention, I couldn't lose myself to music as I normally would during a drive. With the radio turned off, my mind juxtaposed scenes of emptiness and desire. Those were the two things that made it impossible for me to turn around. Though fear had my heart racing, I needed to see this man.

During the ride, I could almost taste his words: "If I have a chance to be around you again, especially if it's the last time, the only thing on my mind will be you. I won't think of anything else." The recollection sent chills reverberating through me. It was the prickling on my skin that continued to fuel my curiosity.

We had never discussed our true intentions. I didn't want to acknowledge that he was every positive thought when my daily life had become so depressing and my relationship so dull. I just couldn't confess that some magic was missing from my life and that he was the only one I felt could bring it back to me. Lord knows that I could never say that I wanted him

45

to have me in every way imaginable, that I wanted to be consumed by the fire that burned every time he was near me. I would become boiling lava, dripping in his presence. I'd lay awake at night trying my best to comprehend how he could bring about such a reaction when we'd never even touched.

Months before this day, we innocently sat together over drinks in order to exchange edited photographs that he had taken of me earlier in the summer. During this meeting, liquid courage and organic discourse led us to admit the apparent energy flowing between us and discuss the sheer danger in spending time together. We sat in this space for hours, sharing dreams and pondering what could have been had we met under different circumstances—like if I didn't have a boyfriend and if he didn't reject monogamy. But the reality was that I did have a man, and to the outside world, we were the very picture of happiness. Posted images on our social media accounts depicted two people in love. I wasn't ready to say that as cute as we appeared to be, the spark was missing. And I certainly wasn't brave enough to face judgment and potential loneliness by leaving someone who was good to me. I sat at that table thinking about how many women dream of having such a man, and there I was smiling in the face of someone else. At the end of our evening together, we agreed to do what any wise adults would do in this situation. We decided to halt all communication, for the sake of my relationship.

For some time, we managed to maintain on the straight and narrow. I threw myself into being the perfect girlfriend and appreciating what I had at home, but I could not stop thinking of him. At work. In the gym. While lying next to my lover. Curiosity nearly drove me insane, and I was almost sure that my boyfriend was beginning to notice my elusiveness when it came to intimacy. I had no desire to be physical with him, using sleepiness and lack of sexual appetite as excuses.

Eventually the sneaking began. Whispered phone conversations. Deleted texts. Private Facebook messages. Near Christmas, we decided that we had to see what it was all about. Had to give in to whatever this thing was and then move on. I could not go on any longer trapped in this abyss of wonder. I could not continue to make my boyfriend suffer by secretly yearning for another man. As crazy as it sounds, I almost felt like I had to see him in the flesh in order to save my relationship. I needed to just get him out of my system.

Now, seven minutes to my destination, no longer could I go back and forth with "what if" questions. I knew I had to go him. There was something so very urgent about it all.

I arrived. Final thoughts of running for my life or going through with this encounter flashed briefly through my mind. I chose the latter. I checked myself out in the mirror, took a deep breath and opened the door to my fate. Walking from the parking garage to the lobby of his apartment, I had the confident strut of a woman who was bold and sure of herself. I liked her. She took the place of the nervous, scared little girl who was in very unfamiliar territory. Thoughts of saving my relationship and feeding my desire strengthened every step as I walked into the lobby.

He came down to get me in a partially buttoned denim shirt and loosely fitting pants, depicting everything I needed in that moment: carefree and uninhibited existence. The water beads on the nape of his neck confirmed that he had just stepped out of the shower. The moisture glistened on the hairs of his thick beard and glossed his rich brown complexion. We walked slowly and quietly to his apartment, neither of us wanting to ruin the moment by saying too many words. In the elevator, we both stole glances, him complimenting the short haircut that displayed my slender neck. His deep voice coupled with a Midwest accent caused me to blush as I said thank you.

Nervous laughter and banter about the fact that I was actually there in his house, filled the living room. A bachelor pad, his space had a minimalist quality. Not many paintings or décor, but it was clean, every piece in its rightful place. What his home lacked in decoration, it made up for in vibes. A speaker system transmitted a blend of minimal hip-hop and R&B to my ears, which worked to relax my nerves and place me deeper in this movie of a moment we were having. Every passing minute confirmed my need to be there. This brother was a dream taking on physicality. We talked about art and aspirations to be genuine creatives as if all of those things could so simply come to pass. A cure for the lack of passion I'd been experiencing, he motivated me to move out of my own way and to just do the shit that I had been yearning to do. He saw through my pretenses and believed in me enough to call me out on my bullshit and ask: "If you're a writer, why aren't you writing?" Then he left me alone on the sofa to consider his question, as he went to prepare a meal for me.

He declined my offer to help him, instead giving me strawberries and a mixed drink of fresh basil, mango, and rye whiskey to busy myself and take the edge off. With each sip of the beverage, all traces of guilt were vanishing. I felt myself opening up and becoming more comfortable as the effects of alcohol and his attractiveness began to work their magic on me. I watched him, maneuvering in the kitchen like a professional. It intrigued me. This man was working overtime for something that I was already mentally preparing to give to him.

Lamb chops had marinated in lemon juice and garlic over night, and now they sizzled in a skillet on the stove next to fresh green beans and sautéed red potatoes. The aroma was intoxicating, further luring me in. He brought the plate of food to me with a smirk on his face, as if he knew exactly what such a dish could to do a woman. He decided that we'd enjoy the meal in his bedroom, and I could not find a reason to deny this. We walked down the hall and finally sat down to eat. Never in my life had I tasted such a tender, succulent, flavorful meat. I closed my eyes as my palate registered the first bite of lamb. A low moan escaped my lips as I chewed. Impeccable. I opened my eyes and looked longingly at him. All of my senses were being tapped into, and I was ready for whatever the evening would bring. I couldn't even finish the meal with such enamor of the moment that this man was giving to me.

Plates discarded in the kitchen, we sat on his full size bed pretending to be engaged in a TV show. He suddenly paused to admire my attire. All black, down to the pantyhose that I wore to shield my thighs from the cold. He rubbed the fabric and bolts of electricity ran through every fiber of my being. Minutes passed as I tried to regain my composure, and then he kissed the back of my neck so softly that I felt myself die a thousand times to the old scared, shelled up version of myself. Again, my eyes closed as my body began to melt. Still caressing my thighs, he pulled off the stockings, down my panties, and bent to taste me. He stopped without warning and gazed at me there, comparing my femininity to a flower. Never had I had a man to savor me as if I was art. I was undone. Before

48

long, we were engaged in an act that didn't feel like dirty cheating, but soft, sweet love making. He held my limbs as if he had been waiting a life time to do so. I was in a trance, in utter disbelief of what I was doing, but oh so wrapped in the moment. I began to release all restraint and give myself to this man fully, at instances taking full control. If indeed, this was to be the first and only experience, I wanted to be filled to the brim. My mind went crazy with the idea that this was not the familiar hands of my love that touched me, yet it was an embrace that I'd craved for months. I was in shock that I could even be enjoying myself. And just as we embarked on a second round and began to find our stride, my phone rang. It was my boyfriend. Mortal terror coursed through every fiber of my being. Instantly, I felt my heart drop to the floor.

Immediately, I was brought to reality with the weight of what was done. Guilt and panic surfaced. My mind scrambled over a lie to tell when my love asked me where I was and what I was doing. I had never been a cheater, and the remorse was more than I could bear. But then I asked myself was it so bad if I was there to save my relationship? And did such a beautiful moment really deserve to be tainted with regret? As I hung up the phone with my trusting boyfriend, my forbidden lover walked up behind me, begging me to come back to bed and stay a little longer. So many parts of me could have remained in rhapsody forever with this man. But, I had to go. Run back to my car. Run back to my man. Run back to the mundane. I didn't even know who I was anymore.

I quickly walked back to the car, my mind coupled with fear of being discovered and gratification of receiving what I'd craved for so long.

The rest of the day felt like an out of body experience. I saw myself greet my boyfriend with a facetious excitement that should have hinted that there was something off with me. I watched myself be hugged and touched by him as if hours ago, I hadn't been lying with another man. I observed the guilt-ridden "I love you," escape my mouth as the clock struck twelve. We welcomed in the New Year together, him thinking that he had found the love of his life and me dreading the day that he ever found out what I did.

That night, I felt like as long as I could keep my indiscretion hidden, we could be happy together. The itch had been scratched. I no longer had to wonder. Days passed and I tried my best to return to the faithful, dedicated woman that I once was. I gave him the intimacy that I'd been holding from him. Cooked his favorite meals and brought him along to parties with my college friends to reassure him that I was in the relationship just as much as he was. I thoroughly tricked myself into believing that I could truly move forward in my relationship, and that the desire for something more had been fulfilled. I told no one of my slip up. Not even my best friend. As far as I was concerned, it didn't exist. But, it did...

Less than a week later, my love discovered my secret. There was uneasiness in the pit of his stomach that wouldn't allow him to accept my erratic behavior on New Year's Eve. When he called, I told him that I was at the gym, yet there was no noise in the background, and I arrived to pick him up fully dressed and appearing to have never broken a sweat. He'd also done enough cheating in his lifetime to know when something just wasn't right. After doing some digging, he confronted me with pain in his eyes, and I watched everything crumble before mine. There was no way to deny any of it. Groveling at his feet, I begged him to stay. I rolled around on the ground, questioning God for my right to live when I'd been so cruel to someone who loved me. I think it was his cool demeanor that messed me up the most. He packed his things, watched television, and made plans to be gone in the morning after the snowfall. He was simply done with me.

It took months of guilt, pity, wallowing, and begging to realize that on the other side of this destruction, there could be freedom.

As much as I wanted to return to normalcy after the affair, life could never really be the same. The damage had been done on the inside. I was around my boyfriend, and still felt the same emptiness. The cheating didn't cure me of anything, as I hoped it would. I found myself still wanting to converse with my lover, wanting to rehash the enchanting moment we shared together. And it wasn't even that I wanted to leave my relationship to be with him. I just ached for something more.

Yet, I was willing to smother all of those emotions due to my fear of uncertainty. I didn't want to find myself single and alone. I kept thinking about how difficult it was to find a good man, especially when I'd experienced so much heartbreak before my boyfriend. I was scared as hell to not have the security that being with him gave to me. He was a sure thing. Nothing that I ever had to question and I felt like I needed that. So, I was willing to pretend and settle in contentment.

The discovery of my wrongdoing, however, made it impossible for me exist in hiding the fact that I craved something deeper. After the tears fell, I had to look at myself in the mirror and admit that I needed more than shacking up with a man in a city that was not my own. I needed more than the disrespect that I faced daily at a job I hated and to not have a man to support me in finding a workplace that did not cause so much stress. I needed much more than sitting around wasting my gifts, feeling completely uninspired and out of place. I needed to feel alive again; I needed fire. I had never been a lukewarm woman, so why was I allowing fear to make that acceptable now? When I cheated, I thought that I was escaping a feeling and feeding an insatiable craving, and before long found that it was so much more. Our breakup was the liberation I needed and perhaps what I was after from the start.

After his initial cold response to my actions, his emotional toll was extreme. Through social media posts and devastating text messages, he expressed his anger and disgust with me. But even through this, he decided to still be with me. Against my own feelings, I felt like I didn't deserve to tell him otherwise when he loved me enough to stay with me. I allowed him to hold it over my head for months. The trust was completely gone, and at any given moment, I was forced to bend over backwards to make him feel secure. He prodded and pushed, and I appeased at every turn, but the relationship eventually came to an end. This was for the best.

There will always be sorrow in my heart for hurting another human being. Night after night, I asked myself why I hadn't been brave enough to just leave it all without the cheating. I've realized that it wasn't about my boyfriend or even about the man outside of my relationship. It was about me needing to never settle and being strong enough to patiently wait for a love that is enough. And that could never truly be found in the bed of another. From my mistakes, came this wisdom and the choice to ask for forgiveness, and offer myself compassion as I journey through this life. Yet, I cannot regret a thing.

IV

Bloom

\ˈblüm\

verb

1.

to produce or yield flowers

2.

 a. (1) to mature into achievement of one's potential (2) to flourish in

beauty, freshness, or excellence

b. to shine out: GLOW

Perception vs. Reality

I.
Perception

You're the one adept in the art of letting go. I've seen you. I see the way they are here one day and gone the next. I see the way you pick yourself up and strut across rooms with your pride intact. I hear them scream your name in the dark and then tell their friends that the reason you're no longer together is because "she only thinks of herself." I witness how you shake their words from your skin. They don't understand how they're unable to break you. I see the luster of the smile that still permeates from your eyes. It's not a façade. I, too, wonder how you do it. From where do you get your power? How do you find the strength to get over?

II.
Reality

What I don't see is how much release drains you. How you tire of making the tough call. How the disappointments prepare you for a breakup before any problem arises. How you have no choice but to listen to the stirring in your spirit. I don't hear the phone calls to your girls that another one bites the dust. Yes, it is true. You are made of the stuff of gods, but you hurt, too.

Reminder #1

Stop waiting on a savior
God has equipped you
with everything
that you need.
Sometimes,
you have to be your own light
at the end of the tunnel.
You have to save yourself.

I Ain't Sorry

This body has changed drastically over the years,
stretching and
spreading
in preparation for what it was created to do.
I can hold life in my belly
and nourish a child on my breast.
This softness is to be worshiped,
these hips exalted.

I will not apologize if
my thickness
makes you
uncomfortable.

Reminder #2

You bend
You curve
You spread
You sustain and release
You share fragrance and spice
You are wide
You are ethnic
You are mine
You are my mother's
You are my grandmother's
And her mother's
And her brother's
And his sister's
And their ancestors
And I am so sorry
for ever
allowing other's opinion
to make me feel
like you were not good enough.
As if God made a mistake.
Let there be no misconception
of the blood
that runs through my veins.
You are just big enough,
just wide enough,
and just open enough
to smell that what they said
is full of shit.

A Headwrap's Ode

Up amongst the heavens, I rest
Wrapping you, complementing you—amazed by you
For a few sacred moments,
I am blessed with the duty
of protecting what the creator has
woven out just for you
your crown of kinks and coils
As your hair is swept away within me,
the emphasis is placed on your face
the face that has stolen the hearts of many men
What an honor it is to witness it,
as it stands alone
with nothing to distract the eye
from the masterpiece it is; it is
my joy to lie upon your head, queen
Perched high as you strut
across whatever continent
you may find yourself in
You woo me at the touch
of your slender fingers to my fibers,
as you twist and tuck me
 into exquisite designs
You no longer care what they think of you,
of how they may perceive your blackness
I love your boldness
and your strength

I am elated it is you who owns me.
With you
I am not simply cloth,
but adornment.

Gratitude

What color would your soul be
without Coltrane
or Basquiat
or Ripperton
or Zora
or Sonia
or Maya?
Mine would most certainly
not be
this beaming yellow,
this dazzling gold.

Maybe, it'd be grey
like clouds before a rain storm,
melancholy and docile
or white
devoid of melanin and magic
or perhaps even black,
unlit and somber.

I thank the creator for those
who have added strokes
to this work of art,
those who have given my spirit its hue.

These Things Do In Remembrance of Me

In my bedroom, there is a bookshelf, and on that shelf, there is a photograph of me around age six, sitting on my father's lap. Not in any other image, can one so accurately point out our resemblance. If you were to pay me a visit on any given afternoon, there'd be a candle burning in front of this frame. There'd also be a miniature replica of his '76 Chevy Chevelle. To you, this is just a shelf, just a picture, and just an unremarkable item. For me, this is an altar.

Everything I do is in his honor.

Grown

Because the bills were coming nonstop
and rent was due
and I was the one
to keep the lights on
and waking up at 5AM to make it to
a real job
I felt like I could have
whoever I wanted in my bed
I mean,
since I paid for it
and I bought the sheets
and I am a grown woman,
with grown woman needs
but somehow having those men
to have me
didn't make me feel real grown
or in control
It made me feel like they could leave
and take a piece of me with 'em
And I don't think I like that.

Reminder #3

It is one thing
to be free
and in control
of your womanhood
and quite another
to share parts of yourself
that you can't get back
with men that you can't keep.
Flaunt your freedom
in the way
that you say no
to anyone
who threatens your peace
and seeks to visit your temple
without plans to worship.

Puzzled

I ran into an old lover yesterday. He embraced me, gazed into my eyes longingly and asked what it was that finally caused me to be done with him.

I replied, "I no longer wished to pick up bits of myself off of dirty floors and piece them back together. I wanted to be whole again."

Reminder #4

Sis,

Sometimes you take life too seriously. The world is not always crashing down around you. You can't help everyone, and there are things you simply cannot change. Calm yourself. Clasp your hands in prayer. Take a deep breath. Release.

Reminder #5

And I know your heart shatters every time potential kisses concrete.
Don't stop believing, though.

Feel It

I once thought that I needed to be the girl who showed strength in her ability to "handle" pain. I relished in the fact that it didn't take me long to mourn the ending of things. Yet, now, I see power in the admittance that "my feelings are hurt by what you did."

Emotions are real and they deserve to be felt. Yet, just as they are alive and breathing, they are fleeting. You are responsible for picking yourself up from that place and moving on. But, you are also human; so, go on, feel it.

Reminder #6

You will be resilient. You will be wise. You will respect yourself and expect it from others. You will inspire multitudes. You will be every magical thing. People will attempt to make a god of you. And then you will turn around and make a choice that completely contradicts everything. You are not perfect. Forgive yourself. Start again.

For My Aries

Don't mistake my passion
for aggression.
Don't think that this fire
is always raging.
Sometimes, I'm slow burn.
Soft flame.
Lantern at dusk.
You need light, right?

Reminder #7

Anything
and everything
must go
that forsakes you—
even parts of you.

For Girls That Buy Themselves Flowers

I desired something beautiful, so I bought myself a bouquet of lilies.

The guy, who was courting me at the time, stopped by, saw them and inquired. He said that I was "something else." He asked why I didn't allow him to do that for me.

I expressed to him that he has to understand the type of woman he's dealing with. Said that I've loved myself for 25 years and even in the moments of not caring for myself properly, I've learned how to stand alone. Told him that it doesn't mean that I won't cherish the flowers he brings, but that I know how to grow and water my own garden.

Because Talk is Cheap

You say that I'm Spring time and your mama's home cooking
rolled all into one?

Make me know it.

Reminder #8

Self-love is not
a road leading to loneliness.
It is not a frivolous whim.
It is not arrogance
nor is it selfishness.
It is not even an option.
It is oxygen.
Water.
You will perish without it.

Reminder #9

We tend to accept and forgive disrespect from our friends that we would never tolerate from the men we date. Stop this.

Full Bloom

He wondered how she came to be so confident, so graceful, so sure of herself. When she walked, she flowed like water through streams. No babies of her own to claim, but he looked inside of her and saw the mother he'd want his daughters to have. She didn't live off of the words that fell from his lips. He admired how she didn't need his existence to breathe. So, he asked her.

She responded: when I was but a child, my mother spoke life over me. She gave me her secrets and her pain. She shared her knowledge. She needed me to know who I was, so she spoke of my magic. She planted lilies in my subconscious. She is the reason.

Reminder #10

You've never met a person or an experience that has been able to break you.

Thank God for this.

Baptism

Sat in a tub of rose water
Soaked until my fingers pruned
Listened to the softest jazz,
fragrant scents of blue sage
and lavender burned through my nostrils
Spirit cleansed, I was full
Laid back my head to revel
in this alchemy, this
calling myself to the altar,
this sanctifying the crown.
Closed my eyes
and felt God on the inside of me
I'd been waiting
for this
sacred breathing.

I recalled intimate moments in showers
water dancing on my skin
as I kissed a man
who I thought made me whole.
Nibbling on my shoulder,
naked as the day we were born.
I could have sworn that one day
I'd carry his seed
and that I'd be whole.
But this?
This is the earth moving.
This is the sun rotating.
This is the ground shaking.
This is the moon glowing.
This is the wave crashing.

This is me.
Whole.
Alone
in a tub
of rose water.
Eyes closed.
Smiling wide as oceans,
with tears in my eyes,
thanking Christ Jesus
for this moment
to baptize my body
and love myself,
deeply.